7848

A New True Book

YOUR FIVE SENSES

By Ray Broekel

This "true book" was prepared under the direction of
William H. Wehrmacher, M.D., FACC, FACP,
Clinical Professor of Medicine and
Adjunct Professor of Physiology,
Loyola University Stritch School of Medicine, Chicago, Illinois,
with the help of his granddaughter Cheryl Sabey

CHILDRENS PRESS ™

CHICAGO

A duck pond has many
sights and sounds.

PHOTO CREDITS

Tony Freeman—2, 4 (bottom left), 6, 7 (4 photos), 10, 16 (2 photos), 21, 25 (2 photos top), 26 (left), 27 (left), 28 (top left), 30 (top and bottom left), 34 (right), 40 (right), 45 (bottom)

Jerry Hennen—4 (top)

Tom Ballard—4 (middle and bottom right), 8, 14 (2 photos), 25 (bottom left), 27 (right), 45 (top left)

Nawrocki Stock Photo—© Jim Whitmer, 32, 42; © Larry Brooks, 26 (right); © Ken Sexton, cover

Hillstrom Stock Photos—© David R. Frazier, 37 (right); ® Richard J. Thorne, 45 (top left)

Lynn Stone—28 (bottom), 30 (bottom right), 45 (top right)

Reinhard Brucker—11, 17, 24, 37 (left), 40 (left), 43 (2 photos)

Joseph A. DiChello—28 (top right), 34 (left), 36, 38

Denoyer-Geppert Co.—23

Phillis Adler—13, 19

Library of Congress Cataloging in Publication Data

Broekel, Ray.
    Your five senses.

    (A New true book)
    Summary: Discusses the importance of the five senses and examines the structure of the sense organs and how they work.
    1. Senses and sensation—Juvenile literature.
[1. Senses and sensation. 2. Sense organs] I. Title.
QP434.B76 1984   612'.8   84-7603
ISBN 0-516-01932-5   AACR2

TABLE OF CONTENTS

All animals
have one or
more senses.

ANIMAL SENSES

Animals have one or more senses. The animal senses are sight, hearing, touch, smell, and taste. Humans and some animals have all five of these senses. Other animals have fewer than five senses. But all animals have one sense—the sense of touch, or feeling.

Some animals may have a sense that is better than

it is in humans. A dog, for
example, has a very good
sense of smell.

Only in humans are all
five senses well developed.
Even though the five
senses are important, a
human can learn to live
without one or more of
them.

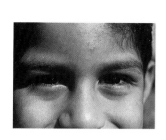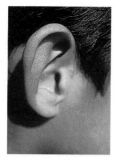

SENSE ORGANS

Different parts of the body are called sense organs. Your eyes and ears let you see and hear. Your skin is a sense organ that responds to the sense of touch. And your nose and tongue are sense organs that let you smell and taste.

SIGHT AND LIGHT

Why do you see a cat?
A tree? Because of light.
Light reflects, or bounces
off, things. That light
travels to your eyes.
Without light there would
be no sight.

Why can you see the
moon? Light from the sun
reflects off the moon. The
light travels to your eyes.
You then see the moon.

Suppose you are in a
room with no doors and
windows. The inside of the
room is as black as the
picture below. Why can't
you see the dog in the

room? Or the ball in the dog's mouth? Because no light is present. Without light you can't see.

Now look at the picture above. Why can you see the dog? Why can you see the ball in its mouth? Light is now present.

Light comes in through the pupil of the eye. It travels through the lens to the back of the eye. At the back is the retina. The retina is a layer of millions of tiny nerve cells. These nerve cells are sensitive to light.

Suppose you are looking at an apple. The eye's lens

focuses light reflected from the apple to the retina. An image of the apple is formed. The image of the apple is then carried to your brain through the optic nerve. You "see" the apple in your brain.

The eye is like a camera. It takes pictures upside down. So you really see things upside down all the time.

The lens forms the image upside down on the

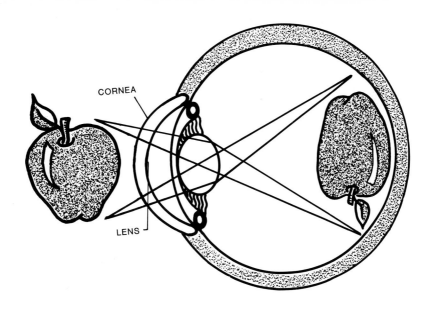

CORNEA

LENS

retina. The upside-down image then travels to the brain through the optic nerve.

Your brain has learned to put things right side up, however. It started doing this when you were a baby.

The images that form on your retina are upside down and reversed left to right.

So thanks to your brain
and your sense of sight,
these girls and boys aren't
jumping rope upside down.

14

HEARING AND SOUND

Why do you hear a radio? A telephone? Because of sound.

Sound is made when something vibrates. To vibrate means to move very, very quickly. A thing may vibrate back and forth, up and down, or from side to side.

When something vibrates, the air around it

Girl (left) listens to the sounds a ruler makes when it vibrates. The telephone sends sound through its wires (above).

also begins to vibrate. This air travels in waves. The waves travel to your ear. And you hear the sound that was made.

The ear has three main parts. They are the outer ear, middle ear, and inner

ear. The outer ear is the part that can be seen.

Suppose a dog barks. How do you hear the sound?

Sound enters the outer ear and travels down a passageway called the ear

canal. At the end of the
ear canal is the eardrum.

The eardrum is a thin
skinlike layer called a
membrane. It is stretched
tightly like a tiny drumhead.
When sound (vibrating air)
hits the eardrum, the
eardrum begins to vibrate.

There are three tiny
bones inside the middle
ear.

The vibration in the
eardrum sets the first bone,
the hammer, in motion. It
causes the second bone, the

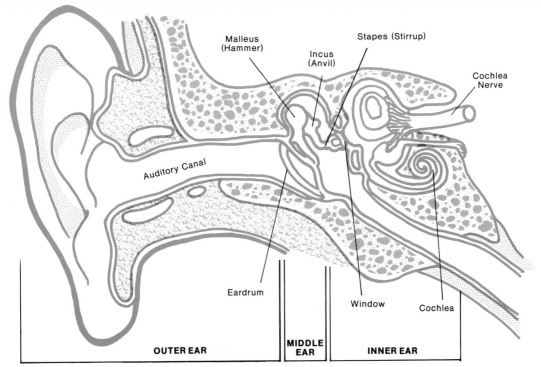

Malleus
(Hammer)

Incus
(Anvil)

Stapes (Stirrup)

Cochlea
Nerve

Auditory Canal

Eardrum

Window

Cochlea

OUTER EAR

**MIDDLE
EAR**

INNER EAR

anvil, to vibrate. Then the
vibration travels to the
last bone, the stirrup. When
the stirrup vibrates it
strikes a membrane in the
middle ear called the
window. The window begins
to vibrate and carries
sound into the inner ear.

The main part of the
inner ear is the cochlea.
The cochlea is filled with a
liquid. When the middle-ear
window begins to vibrate,
the liquid is put into
motion. These vibrations
move from the liquid
through a membrane to
tiny hairlike sound cells.
   The sound message
goes from those cells to

the auditory nerve. The auditory nerve carries the sound message to the brain. And you hear the dog bark!

THE SENSE OF TOUCH

You are in a dark room
and bump into something
hard. You put out a hand
to touch and feel the thing.
You find out what it is
very quickly. You say, "I
just bumped into a chair."

Which of your senses
helped with the answer?
Your sense of touch.

All of the skin is a
sense organ. Skin has
thousands of tiny nerves.
These nerves make up

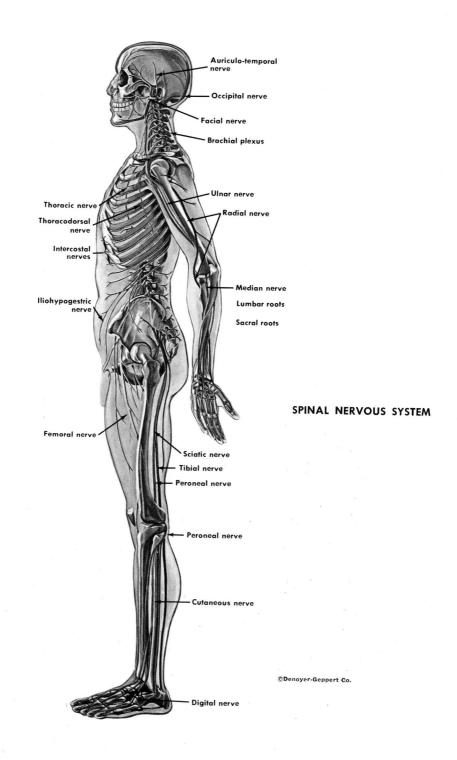

Auriculo-temporal nerve

Occipital nerve

Facial nerve

Brachial plexus

Thoracic nerve

Thoracodorsal nerve

Intercostal nerves

Ulnar nerve

Radial nerve

Median nerve

Lumbar roots

Sacral roots

Iliohypogestric nerve

SPINAL NERVOUS SYSTEM

Femoral nerve

Sciatic nerve

Tibial nerve

Peroneal nerve

Peroneal nerve

Cutaneous nerve

©Denoyer-Geppert Co.

Digital nerve

smaller groups of sense organs. And they send messages to the brain.

Some nerves respond to pressure. You felt pressure when you bumped into the chair. You touched and felt it to find out what it was.

Nerves in your skin allow you to feel things.

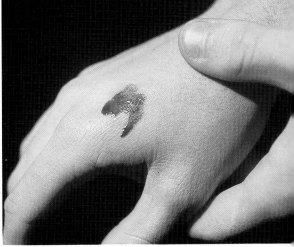

Your nerves send signals to your brain. Your brain tells you when something is cold, hot, or painful. Your body will react to each of these sensations.

Other tiny nerves are sense organs that respond to pain. Others respond to heat, and still others to cold.

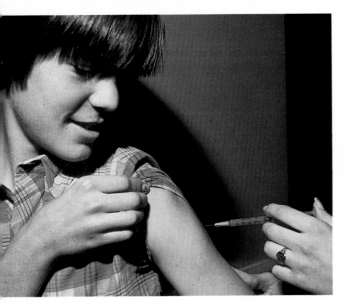

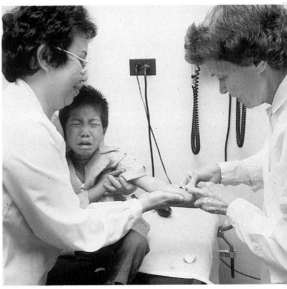

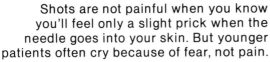
Shots are not painful when you know
you'll feel only a slight prick when the
needle goes into your skin. But younger
patients often cry because of fear, not pain.

A nurse gives you a
shot. You feel it when the
needle pricks your skin.
Why? The tiny nerve sense
organs respond and send
messages to your brain.
And you feel the needle.

At the beach you run
across some hot sand. You
feel the heat when your
feet touch the sand.

You take out a can of
cola that has been on ice.
The can feels cold to the
touch.

The tiny nerve sense organs in your skin are much closer together in your fingers than in your shoulders.

The tiny nerve sense organs are all over your skin, from your head to your toes. In some places they are closer together than in others.

For example, they are closer in your fingertips than in your forearms. But close together or far apart, they still tell your brain whether something is hot, warm, cool, cold, hard, soft, smooth, rough, or sharp.

THE SENSE OF SMELL

Freshly baked chocolate chip cookies—what a wonderful smell they have! What about the smell in the air just after a spring shower? Great! Or the odor of a bunch of roses? Nice.

But then, what about the smell of a fish that is no longer fresh? Phew! What about the odor coming

from a garbage can? Not
so good. Or the odor given
off by an angry skunk?
Awful!

Things that give off
odors release chemicals
that may be gases or tiny
drops of liquid. Some
things give them off when
they are crushed, broken,

or heated. The odors travel through the air. When they reach your nose, things happen.

Inside the membrane of your nose are nerve endings. There are lots of them. They are very sensitive to smells. And they are all connected to the olfactory nerves. The olfactory nerves carry smell messages to your brain.

Those smell messages reach that part of your

brain that identifies
different kinds of smells.
Your brain then lets you
know what you have been
sniffing. If it is bad you
might soon be frowning.
But if the smell is good
you'll smile.

THE SENSE OF TASTE

Find a mirror. Now stick your tongue out at yourself. Look closely at your tongue. See those tiny bumps all over it? Each bump contains a nerve ending. And each nerve ending is shaped like a tiny cup. It is called a taste bud. The taste buds on your tongue can tell the differences in taste among things you eat.

Taste buds respond to
things that are sweet, salty,
sour, or bitter. All the
things you taste are made
up of one or more of
those four tastes.

Sweet and salty things
are tasted near the tip of

the tongue. Why? Because
most taste buds that
respond to sweet and salty
things are located there.
Sour things are tasted at
the sides. And most taste
buds that respond to bitter
things are at the back of
the tongue.

To be tasted, things need to be dissolved. For example, the sweet taste of sugar comes out when sugar dissolves on taste buds. The sugar mixes

In a pie eating contest you eat so fast you hardly have time to taste the pie.

with saliva. Saliva is a watery liquid in the mouth. It causes sugar to dissolve. Then the sweetness of sugar can be tasted.

There are some things that really can't be tasted unless they also can be smelled. The two senses of taste and smell work together to identify them.

Suppose you have a cold. Your nose is so stopped up that you can't

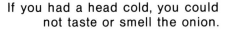
If you had a head cold, you could
not taste or smell the onion.

smell. You take a bite of
food without looking at it.
Can you tell just by tasting
it that it was a piece of
onion? No, because your
sense of smell isn't
working. So you cannot
identify it as an onion.

40

As a baby you could not identify the tastes of different things. As you grew older, however, you became used to the tastes of many different things and could identify them.

You cannot taste things too well if they are very hot or very cold. Taste buds work best if things are at room temperature.

Taste buds also work best at identifying foods

eaten one at a time. It is
easy to identify a piece of
apple or an orange slice.

But it is hard to pick out
all the tastes in foods that
have many different items,
like a bowl of vegetable
soup.

Taste buds work best if foods are at room
temperature—neither too hot nor too cold.

USING YOUR SENSES

Make good use of the senses of sight, hearing, touch, smell, and taste. But also use another kind of sense whenever you use the five senses.

It's called common sense. Common sense has to do with how you think and act. When you think and act wisely, then you are using common sense.

You'll be using common
sense if you pay attention
to what you see, hear,
touch, smell, and taste.

WORDS YOU SHOULD KNOW

anvil(AN • vil) — a bone of the middle ear

auditory nerve(AW • dih • tor • ee NERV) — nerve having to do with the sense of hearing

brain(BRAYNE) — chief nerve center in the skull of a human or animal

chemical(KEM • ih • kil) — substance made by or used in a chemical process

cochlea(COCK • lee • ah) — small hollow organ in the inner ear

dissolve(diss • OLVE) — to make or become a liquid

ear canal(EER kah • NAL) — passageway through which sound travels in the outer ear to the eardrum

eardrum(EER • drum) — thin membrane stretched tightly inside the ear; transmits sound waves to the inner ear

hammer(HAM • er) — a bone of the middle ear

hearing(HEER • ing) — the sense by which sounds are experienced

image(IM • ij) — a likeness

lens(LENZ) — transparent part of the eye that serves to focus an image on the retina

membrane(MEM • brain) — a thin, flexible layer of tissue that covers or lines certain organs

nerve(NERV) — any of the fibers or bunch of fibers that carry impulses between the brain or spinal cord and all parts of the body

nerve cell(NERV SELL) — the basic cell unit of a nerve

olfactory nerves(ohl • FAK • ter • ee NERVZ) — nerves having to do with the sense of smell

optic nerve(OP • tik NERV) — nerve having to do with the sense of sight

pressure(PRESH • er) — the act of pressing or the condition of being pressed upon

pupil(PYOO • pil) — the dark central part of the eye through which light is admitted

reflect(ree • FLEKT) — to throw or cast back, bounce off

retina(RETT • nah) — layer of cells at the back of the eye sensitive to light

saliva(sah • LIVE • ah) — a watery liquid in the mouth

sense(SENSS) — one of the bodily or mental powers by which a person is made aware of the world outside, as sight, hearing, touch, smell, and taste

sense organ(SENSS OR • gan) — a body part, such as the nose, tongue, skin, eyes, or ears, that responds to a given sense

sight(SITE) — the act of seeing

smell(SMELL) — the act of smelling

sound(SOUND) — anything that can be heard

stirrup(STER • up) — a bone of the inner ear

taste(TAYST) — to identify the flavor of something by taking it into the mouth

taste bud(TAYST BUD) — a special cell sensitive to taste

touch(TUTCH) — to come into contact with something

vibrate(VYE • brate) — to quickly move back and forth, up and down, or side to side

wave(WAIVE) — any energy, as light or sound, that exists in pulses or alternations of one kind or another

window(WIN • doh) — a membrane in the inner ear

INDEX

About the Author

Ray Broekel is a full-time freelance writer who lives with his wife, Peg, and a dog, Fergus, in Ipswich, Massachusetts. He has had twenty years of experience as a children's book editor and newspaper supervisor, and has taught all subjects in kindergarten through college levels. Dr. Broekel has had over 1,000 stories and articles published, and over 100 books. His first book was published in 1956 (it was published by Childrens Press).